LOVING
Your Wife

*How to
Strengthen
Your Marriage
in a Fallen
World*

W9-BSQ-521

A Bible Study for Men by
Jack & Cynthia Heald

NAVPRESS®
Bringing Truth to Life

OUR GUARANTEE TO YOU

We believe so strongly in the message of our books that we are making this quality guarantee to you. If for any reason you are disappointed with the content of this book, return the title page to us with your name and address and we will refund to you the list price of the book. To help us serve you better, please briefly describe why you were disappointed. Mail your refund request to: NavPress, P.O. Box 35002, Colorado Springs, CO 80935.

The Navigators is an international Christian organization. Our mission is to reach, disciple, and equip people to know Christ and to make Him known through successive generations. We envision multitudes of diverse people in the United States and every other nation who have a passionate love for Christ, live a lifestyle of sharing Christ's love, and multiply spiritual laborers among those without Christ.

NavPress is the publishing ministry of The Navigators. NavPress publications help believers learn biblical truth and apply what they learn to their lives and ministries. Our mission is to stimulate spiritual formation among our readers.

FOR A FREE CATALOG OF
NAVPRESS BOOKS & BIBLE STUDIES,
CALL 1-800-366-7788 (USA).
IN CANADA, CALL 1-416-499-4615.

CONTENTS

AUTHOR

Jack M. Heald, Jr., is a native Texan. He and his wife, Cynthia, live in Tucson, Arizona, and are the parents of four children: Melinda, Daryl, Shelly, and Michael.

Jack graduated from Texas A & M University with a degree in veterinary medicine. After practicing as a veterinarian for seventeen years, he joined the staff of The Navigators and now ministers to businessmen, pastors, and athletes. He also enjoys teaching marriage and parenting seminars with Cynthia, author of the popular Bible studies *Becoming a Woman of Excellence, Becoming a Woman of Freedom, Intimacy with God,* and *Loving Your Husband,* and the daily devotional *Abiding in Christ.*

PREFACE

I have written this study because I believe a man's greatest needs are to know God intimately and to trust in His faithful Word. As Adam's offspring we, too, live out of Eden, but not out of God's plan. Since marriage is the Lord's plan for most men, we should study God's design and instructions for being a godly husband.

I pray that the study of Scripture as it relates to you and your marriage will be as special to you as it has been to me. God is continuing to teach me daily how to love Cynthia and how to be loved. My desire is for you to learn to love your wife and to live together as "joint heirs of the grace of life." As an overflow of this life you will teach your children and other men to do the same.

> Brethren, I do not regard myself as having laid hold of it yet; but one thing I do: forgetting what lies behind and reaching forward to what lies ahead, I press on toward the goal for the prize of the upward call of God in Christ Jesus. (Philippians 3:13-14)

> Keep pressin' on.

SUGGESTIONS FOR
HOW TO USE THIS STUDY

The purpose of *Loving Your Wife* is to help you understand how to become a godly husband in today's world. Through exploring key scripture passages, reflecting on your personal situation, and considering the insights of godly writers, you will have opportunity to discover biblical truth and apply it in the joys as well as the struggles of your life as a married man.

You'll come across the following sections in each lesson:

Insight into Scripture. This part of your study will take you to key scriptures relevant to the topic at hand. Keep in mind that reference aids—such as a study Bible, a general commentary, a Bible dictionary—can greatly assist you in understanding and interpreting God's Word. You will also need access to a standard dictionary to help you define key words and concepts.

Insight into myself. Here you will be asked to reflect on your attitudes and circumstances in order to examine areas of your life addressed by a given chapter.

Be honest and thoughtful; the purpose of this section is simply to help you understand yourself. You may want to keep some of these answers between yourself and the Lord, or share them with one close friend. Answer them based on the way you are, not on the way you think you should be. Remember that becoming a godly husband is a lifelong process through God's work in you.

As you approach these questions, pray for God's wisdom in revealing to you those aspects of your behavior or perspectives in which He desires you to be especially open to the work of His Holy Spirit.

Insight into my wife. This group of questions will deepen your awareness of how you and your spouse relate to each other by asking you to reflect on issues from your wife's point of view.

Your answers here will complement the insights you uncover about yourself, and they may also reveal areas in which you need to know more about how your wife thinks or what she feels. If you don't know and can't guess at an answer, consider asking your wife for her response, if you feel the freedom to do so. This could open up some healthy communication and provide you both with a "good excuse" for talking over some things you might otherwise not have gotten around to discussing.

Insight from an older man. In this section you'll find a personal reflection from Jack, often with an anecdote to help you learn from his life experiences. This part of the study, which contains challenges, encouragements, explanations, cautions—even confessions!—gives you the chance to follow the friendly voice of a man who has been across this territory already and can help point the way.

Included throughout this study are excerpts from godly and insightful writers on the marriage relationship. Use them to stimulate your thinking, reinforce what you're learning, and enhance your understanding in those areas that seem particularly troublesome or uncertain to you.

This study has been designed for you to use individually or in a group. The companion study for wives, *Loving Your Husband* (available from NavPress), is also designed for individual or group use. The two studies have enough common material and focus to be used together, and are flexible enough to be used in several different ways. Here are some ideas:

1. Use *Loving Your Wife* on your own, perhaps

choosing a trusted male friend with whom to share your responses.

2. Go through *Loving Your Wife* in a small group composed of married men. Rotate leadership and place the emphasis on sharing experiences, insights, reactions, questions, etc. as you provide encouragement, challenge, accountability, and prayer support for each other.

3. Work through *Loving Your Wife* while your wife works through *Loving Your Husband*. Share your responses with each other and discuss what you're learning and how you're reacting to the insights offered by the author and the writers quoted. Since the lessons in each study work together but can also stand alone, you and your wife could select only those lessons you feel would be most beneficial if you decide not to go through the whole study all in one period of time.

4. Go through these two studies in a mixed small group of couples. This arrangement could be very stimulating, but because of the many variables involved (husbands and wives, two different studies) you would need to plan carefully and structure your time for maximum benefit. The group would most likely function more effectively if members knew each other and had established at least some level of rapport before your sessions started. Leadership of the group could be assigned to either couples or individuals.

You might consider having each couple go over their lessons with each other at home before meeting with the group. Or, when you convene, first break up the group into smaller groups of all husbands and of all wives. Then get everyone together for a summary from each contingent regarding major questions and insights, followed by general group discussion.

Of course, you could simply open up the group each time with an open-ended, free-for-all discussion of whatever members wanted to go over, but you would need an especially competent group leader well-versed in the art of controlling, stimulating, and moderating group discussion and interaction. With both husbands and wives present, and two different studies from which to draw, you would probably not run out of things to talk about in an average session.

Sprinkling an occasional purely-social outing into a group like this could enliven your fellowship with each other, create a more comfortable environment for regular sessions, and provide husbands and wives with an outlet for spending some recreational time together in a group context.

No matter how you use this study, above all pray for God's guidance and grace in using it to make you a husband more fully devoted to glorifying Him.

"Whom Have I in Heaven But You?"

Whom have I in Heaven but You? And I have no delight or desire on earth beside You. My flesh and my heart may fail, but God is the rock and firm strength of my heart, and my portion for ever.
Psalm 73:25-26 (AMP)

And all we need to live as Christians, no matter what our circumstances, is the security of His love and the significance of participation in His purpose. We must never claim that our relationships with others do not affect us deeply: they do. But Christ's resources are enough to keep us going.[1]
Lawrence J. Crabb, Jr.

"No one told me that after marriage came life!" "After moonlight and roses, come daylight and dishes." These are great commentaries on the reality of marriage. Larry Crabb states that many of us stand at the altar and silently repeat the vow, "I give myself to you for the rest of my life for you to meet all of my needs." We all have profound, demanding needs that cry to be satisfied. Naively, we think that if we marry, all our needs will be met. It wasn't long after we were married that Cynthia and I had our first disagreement. I remember smiling and saying, "Well, the honeymoon must be over!" All too soon, we realize that the "honeymoon" cannot last forever and that we are still individuals with specific needs. If these needs cannot be fully satisfied in marriage, then where do we go with our feelings of wanting to be loved and to be accepted as someone of value?

Insight into Scripture

1. Nicodemus was a ruler of the Jews, a member of the Sanhedrin (the Jewish ruling council). He came to Jesus to question Him. Read John 3:1-8 and answer the following questions.

   a. How did Nicodemus approach Jesus? *by night — called Him Rabbi, God is with you.*

   b. How did Jesus answer Nicodemus? *Jesus said truly you must be Born again to see the Kingdom of God.*

   c. What does Jesus' response mean to you? *This is more than something of work to do. This is a spiritual Birth.*

d. Why do you think Nicodemus came to talk with Jesus? *He saw Jesus's signs and miracles, He had questions He wanted answered.*

---

2. As a result of Jesus' discourse on His being man's exclusive provision for eternal life, many of His disciples withdrew from Him (John 6:41-66). Read John 6:67-69 and respond to the questions below.

   a. As the remaining disciples observed other men turning away from following Jesus, what was the Lord's question to them?

   b. What was Peter's reply?

   c. What is your response to the Lord's question?

---

3. As the Lord becomes our source of refreshment and nourishment for our spirits, we become secure in who we are in Christ. After studying the following verses, write down the thoughts conveyed in these scriptures concerning God's sufficiency in our lives.

   Psalm 27:1

   Psalm 56

Psalm 62:1-2

Colossians 2:9-10

Colossians 3:1-3

---

4. When we are depending upon the Lord to meet our deepest needs, Paul's words found in Philippians 2:3-4 and 4:4-7 take on new meaning. Study these passages and write a paragraph summarizing your thoughts on how these verses speak to you as a man in Christ who is married.

> Until I am born again and begin to see the Kingdom of God, I see along the line of my prejudices only; I need the surgical operation of external events and an internal purification. It must be God first, God second, and God third, until the life is faced steadily with God and no one else is of any account whatever. "In all the world there is none but thee, my God, there is none but thee."[2]
> Oswald Chambers

Insight into myself

5. It is important that we examine ourselves and understand how we respond to our wives. Throughout this study as you come to this section in each lesson, ponder and pray over these questions designed to reveal your attitudes and your particular circumstances.

   a. How would I describe my deepest needs and longings?

   b. How do I tend to satisfy my needs? On whom do I depend?

   c. How do I think God views my dependence on Him?

   d. When I feel that my wife has failed to meet my needs, how do I react? What do I do when she fails me?

   e. How can I begin to experience more of God's sufficiency in my life?

For one of the most profound ways in which the Lord touches us and teaches us about Himself and His own essential *otherness* is through the very limits He has placed upon our relationships with one another. It is an enormous source of human frustration that our need for intimacy far outstrips its capacity to be met in other people. Primarily what keeps us separate is our sin, but there is also another factor, and that is that in each one of us the holiest and neediest and most sensitive place of all has been made and is reserved for God alone, so that only He can enter there. No one else can love us as He does, and no one can be the sort of Friend to us that He is.[3]

Mike Mason

Insight into my wife

6. In order to gain greater insight into your marriage, carefully consider these questions concerning your wife's attitudes and perspectives. This section occurs in each lesson and will complement the insights you discover about yourself. If you're not sure how your wife would answer, and if you feel free to do so, you might ask her what her answer would be.

a. What are my wife's deepest needs and longings?

b. In what ways do I minister to her needs?

18

c. Does my wife feel that she measures up to my expectations of a "good wife"? Why or why not?

d. What is one change I can make to deepen my sensitivity and ministry to my wife?

Husbands and wives are to regard marriage as an opportunity to minister in a unique and special way to another human being, to be used of God to bring their spouses into a more satisfying appreciation of their worth as persons who are secure and significant in Jesus Christ.[4]

Lawrence J. Crabb, Jr.

Insight from an older man

A short time after we were married I was faced with circumstances that made me realize that Cynthia was not going to meet all of my "needs"—whatever they seemed to be at the moment. I felt I had needs that I couldn't or wouldn't express, but I still remember expecting her to know what they were! The honeymoon was over for me when I realized that she wasn't the perfect wife. It was not encouraging, also, to recognize that I was falling short of what she had in mind for an ideal husband. Like many men in relationships, I had difficulty talking to her about how I felt. I didn't turn to God at this time because I felt that God was for older people, or mainly women! I was looking for "something more" in every area of my life, so I began to get more involved in business, sports, and community activities, hoping that my needs would be met.

Because I wanted to have some common interests with Cynthia I reluctantly attended a couples' Bible study.

There I met some prominent businessmen who were very serious about the Christian faith, yet they seemed to have fun at the same time. After talking to these men and reading the Scriptures for myself, just like Nicodemus I came to Jesus at night and was born again. Studying the Bible led me to a greater understanding of how God desired to be all I need, and this freed me from demanding that other things, other people, or even Cynthia must meet my need for unconditional love and fulfillment. As Peter essentially said, "Where else can anyone go, but to the Lord?"

We ought to be comfortable to live with, because we are not demanding, but understanding. Controlled by Jesus Christ, we are free from obsession with self, and can listen, love, and pray.

Our basic fulfillment does not come from marriage, from prestige, from position, or from possessions. It comes as we are so indwelt by God that his fellowship meets our inner need and we experience the outworking of his love through us.[5]
Gladys M. Hunt

Suggested Scripture memory: Psalm 73:25-26

NOTES
1. Lawrence J. Crabb, Jr., *The Marriage Builder* (Grand Rapids: Zondervan Publishing House, 1982), page 36.
2. Oswald Chambers, *My Utmost for His Highest* (New York: Dodd, Mead & Company, 1966), page 195.
3. Mike Mason, *The Mystery of Marriage* (Portland, Oreg.: Multnomah Press, 1985), page 33.
4. Crabb, page 52.
5. Gladys M. Hunt, "She Has No Equal," in *The Marriage Affair,* J. Allan Petersen, ed. (Wheaton, Ill.: Tyndale House Publishers, 1971), page 96.

"Unless the Lord Builds the House"

Unless the LORD builds the house,
they labor in vain who build it.
Psalm 127:1

Until I am aware that my needs
are already met in Christ, I will
be motivated by emptiness to
meet my needs. When by simple
faith I accept Christ's shed blood
as full payment for my sins, I am
brought into a relationship with
an infinite Being of love and
purpose who fully satisfies my
deepest needs for security and
significance. Therefore I am
freed from self-centered
preoccupation with my own
needs; they are met. It is now
possible for me to give to others
out of my fullness rather than
needing to receive from others
because of my emptiness. For the
first time, I have the option of
living selflessly.[1]
Lawrence J. Crabb, Jr.

A man who understands what is true, right, and lasting creates and establishes a home for his wife and family where security, encouragement, and peace dwell. God has given men the knowledge of Himself in the Scriptures, and the Holy Spirit gives us the understanding we need. Wisdom is defined as "the skill in living." A wise man seeks God's guidance, strength, and wisdom in being the man, the husband, the father he should be. It is difficult for us as men to do this, however, because it involves letting God teach us His character, and it means allowing the Lord to build our homes. It is accepting "the option of living selflessly."

Insight into Scripture

1. Proverbs 9:9 states, "Give instruction to a wise man, and he will be still wiser."

   a. What instructions are communicated in the following verses about some necessary spiritual commitments in order to become wise?

   Luke 6:46-49 *HEARING JESUS WORDS AND doing Them.*

   Luke 14:25-30 *must Hate father & mother, wife and children, brothers and sisters and his own life, bear own Cross and come after me.*

   2 Corinthians 5:14-15 *the love of Christ constrains us, one Died for all, than all died we are not to live for our selfs.*

   2 Timothy 2:15 *I must be diligent. a worker not ashame, able to rightly dividing the word of truth*

22

b. How would each of these commitments help you in becoming wise? *spiritual commitment, Turning from self to Jesus, not living for self but for Christ. being diligent and a worker. Knowing the word aright*

---

2. Proverbs 2:6 states, "For the LORD gives wisdom; from His mouth come knowledge and understanding."

a. Read Psalm 119:97-105 and write down the psalmist's various responses to God's Word.

my meditation all the day. wiser than my enemies. I have understanding, than my Teachers. your testomonies are my meditations. more understanding than the ancients, I keep your precepts. my feet turned from evil way! you taught me. I keep your word your world are sweeter than Honey.

b. How does this passage encourage you to strengthen your walk with the Lord and to grow in wisdom?

because somuch is to be learned from Davids responses, I know as I study these psalms I to can start having the some resposes.

---

3. a. Proverbs 24:3-4 provides a verbal picture of building a house. Study these verses carefully (you might consult a dictionary and/or a commentary) and write down your thoughts about how wisdom, understanding, and knowledge contribute to building a house.

Knowledge is the begining of wisdom wisdom comes from God a lack of Knowledge causes one to perish. Get wisdom also get understanding. the Fear of the Lord is the Begining of Knowledge.

23

b. Refer to Proverbs 11:29. If a house is built by wisdom, in what ways can a man "trouble" his home? Describe this man's inheritance.

will inherit the wind.

---

4. The wise man portrayed in Proverbs 1 is secure because he fears the Lord. Proverbs 1:7 reminds us that "the fear of the LORD is the beginning of knowledge." This proper reverence and respect for the living God can be an essential motivating factor in our becoming wise.

a. What insights about how we build can be found in 1 Corinthians 3:10-15? *Jesus is the foundation we need to take Heed How we build. we need to use right materials. our works will be on Display. Same as by Fire*

b. In what ways does this passage speak to you about the importance of how we build with our lives? (You might want to define gold, silver, and precious stones, and wood, hay, and stubble.) *Gold, silver and stones will stand the Test of Fire. wood, Hay, and stubble will all burn up.*

> If you really believe, as David Livingstone said, that God's promise is the word of a Gentleman of the most strict and sacred honor, then your overall perspective has to be positive. He enables for what he asks. His promises are enough for the problems. His building of the house assures us that our labor will not be in vain.[2]
>
> J. Allan Petersen

5. a. How do I view the cost involved in becoming a wise man? *There are no short cuts to wisdom. Jesus said He is a pear of great price. Sell all and buy from Him.*

b. Practically speaking, what do I do daily to gain wisdom? *Reverence the Lord and stay in the word.*

c. What are some specific ways I build in gold, silver, and precious stones? *Dying to self, and doing for others, giving with a cheerful heart, do everything as unto the Lord.*

d. What is there in my life that produces wood, hay, and stubble? What can I do to begin to minimize this part of my life? *Serving self, doing things for self, having the wrong motivations, talking one thing, but doing another.*

e. If it is your goal to be a wise man, write out a prayer of commitment to the Lord expressing your feelings and desires. *Insight from an older man I take this as my prayer, and commitment to God. This also expresses my feelings and desires.*

> Keep at the Source, guard well your belief in Jesus Christ and your relationship to Him, and there will be a steady flow for other lives, no dryness and no deadness.[3]
>
> Oswald Chambers

---

6. a. Is my wife able to discern my growth in Christlike-
   ness? Why or why not? *yes because of our life Style our desire to obey and do the will of God.*

   b. In what ways is she aware of my desire to build her
   up so that she is encouraged and affirmed? *I Pray with Her, also Study with Her I encourage Her to read the word. I tell Her she is important to Gods Kingdom He loves Her.*

   c. How would my wife describe the way I "build" our
   home? Why? *she would Say its built on The word, and God's promises.*

   d. What, if anything, is something I know she would
   like me to do differently in relation to her or to our
   home? *prepar ahead for Special Days in Her life, and do things to Suprise Her*

> The Lord alone can give you these skills and abilities.
> You can't do it on your own. Working independently
> of Him will accomplish zero. Frustration and futility
> will haunt you if you try to do it in your own strength.
> Remember, it is the Lord who gives these gifts. Unless
> the Lord pulls it off, you labor in vain.[4]
> Charles R. Swindoll

Insight from an older man

To be skilled in any trade involves a lifelong commitment
to excellence, not just a short apprenticeship. I want to be
a workman approved by God in my knowledge of and skill

in applying His principles to my life and marriage. All of this requires time, discipline, and perseverance. In 1964 I asked God to show me how His Word was valuable for my life twenty-four hours a day, seven days a week. What little I know now has been more than adequate. I want to know more of Him, and I want Him to be my source of wisdom to build, establish, and fill my life, marriage, and home. I am excited at the prospect that men today can have the vision for their lives that Ezra, the prophet, had: "For Ezra has set his heart to study the law of the Lord, and to practice it, and to teach His statutes and ordinances in Israel" (Ezra 7:10). I know that I want my teaching to be first by the example of a commitment to God and to my marriage.

He who fears the LORD has a secure fortress,
and for his children it will be a refuge.
Proverbs 14:26 (NIV)

Suggested Scripture memory: Proverbs 24:3-4

NOTES
1. Lawrence J. Crabb, Jr., *The Marriage Builder* (Grand Rapids: Zondervan Publishing House, 1982), page 57.
2. J. Allan Petersen, quoted in *The Marriage Affair* (Wheaton, Ill.: Tyndale House Publishers, 1971), page 5.
3. Oswald Chambers, *My Utmost for His Highest* (New York: Dodd, Mead & Company, 1966), page 251.
4. Charles R. Swindoll, *Strike the Original Match* (Portland, Oreg.: Multnomah Press, 1980), page 25.

"It Is Not Good for the Man to Be Alone"

Then the LORD God said, "It is not good for the man to be alone; I will make him a helper suitable for him."

Genesis 2:18

That the woman was made of a rib out of the side of Adam; not made out of his head to rule over him, nor out of his feet to be trampled upon by him, but out of his side to be equal with him, under his arm to be protected, and near his heart to be beloved.[1]

Matthew Henry

When the Lord brought Eve to Adam, the Living Bible says that Adam responded by saying, "This is it!" In God's creation we recognize His plan for marriage and the family. The Lord said, "It is not good for the man to be alone." In His wisdom God gives us wives to complete us, to help us, and to be our compan- ions for our benefit. As husbands, we must remember to view our wives as the helpers God intended them to be in our lives.

Insight into Scripture

1. After creating Adam, God placed him in the garden. Genesis 2:15-25 provides a detailed account of Eve's creation. Read this passage and use the questions below to help you think creatively about God's pur- poses in these events.

   a. Why do you think God gave the command found in verses 16-17 to Adam before He created Eve?

   He was the head Priest, the first Human created by God

   b. Express your thoughts concerning why God said, "It is not good for the man to be alone" (verse 18).

   adam wasent Complet by Him self. God made Him male & female

   c. Define: *There was a woman in him*

   helper— *One who helps also completes*

   suitable— *a lot like Him, but not the same.*

   d. Describe how Adam might have felt when he realized that there was not a partner suitable for him (verse 20).

   I believe He was wondering why in all that God had made, there was not one that 30 was comparable to Him. He must have thought am I the only one of my kind—

e. Why do you think God waited to create Eve?

I believe God always does Things in Divine Order this was God's order of Things

f. What does "become one flesh" mean to you (verse 24)?

It means that two peppl can be one, and at the same time be Diffient, or their own Selfs.

The Lord God made woman out of part of man's side and closed up the place with flesh, but in marriage He reopens this empty, aching place in man and begins the process of putting the woman back again, if not literally *in* the side, then certainly *at* it: permanently there, intrusively there, a sudden lifelong resident of a space which until that point the man will have considered to be his own private territory, even his own body. But in marriage he will cleave to the woman, and the woman to him, the way his own flesh cleaves to his own bones.

Just so, says the Lord, do I Myself desire to invade your deepest privacy, binding you to Me all your life long and even into eternity with cords of blood.[2]

Mike Mason

---

2. a. Proverbs mentions a wife's usefulness in descriptive terms. What do the following scriptures say about wives?

Proverbs 12:4 *An excellent wife is the Crown of Her Husband; But she who causes shame is like rotteness in His Bones.*

Proverbs 18:22 *He who finds a wife finds a Good thing, and Obtains Favor of the Lord.*

Proverbs 19:14 *Houses and riches are an Inheritance from the Father, but a prudent wife is from the Lord.*

1. a good wife is a Crown of the Husband.
2. finding a Good wife is also finding Favor of the Lord. blessed is the
3. Husban who has a Prudent wife
4. The wife can also cause shame To her Husband

b. Write a brief summary of the key thoughts these proverbs express. *a wife is a Crown of the Husband. also Two people are one, and Different at the same time. a Prudent wife is from the Lord. finding a good wife is finding Favor of the Lord.*

3. The Scriptures give instances of <u>wives providing</u> <u>needed counsel, help, and creative ideas.</u> Read the verses below and write down how the wife was a help to her husband.

Judges 13:15-23 (Before verse 15, Manoah and his wife were given a message concerning the birth of their son, Samson, by the angel of the Lord.) *she gave counsel to Her Husband, and That god had accepted their offering she reminded Him of the good news they received.*

2 Kings 4:8-10 *she ask of Her Husband if they Could make a place where He Could Stay. she recognized Him as a man of God.*

Acts 18:1-3,24-26 *Paul found lodging with a Husband & wife Team who was also Tent makers*

God adds that the one He would bring alongside Adam would be "suitable for him." Literally, "corresponding to" him. She would provide those missing pieces from the puzzle of his life. She would complete him as a qualified, corresponding partner. It is a beautiful picture of a dignified, necessary role filled by one whom God would make and bring alongside the man. In God's original design the plan was to have each partner distinct and unique, needing each other and therefore finding fulfillment with each other.[3]

Charles R. Swindoll

Insight into myself

4. a. Do I basically view my wife as a companion suitable
   for me? Why or why not? *She may not always.
   feel like doing all the things I want, but
   she does them just the same.*

   b. How do I allow my wife to be a help to me?
   *I ask Her what she think about certain
   things, and then I listen to Her suggestions*

   c. Do I tend to expect or demand too much from my
   wife? Explain. *I do some of the time because I some times move to fast for
   Her.*

   d. How do I regard my wife's counsel on finances, job
   changes, or major moves? *I value Her Counsel
   Very much. even at times we don't
   always agree.*

We are not alone when it comes to other people, and
neither are we alone when it comes to God. However
much we may wish at times to be left alone, it is not
an option. It is the one thing which God and marriage
refuse to allow us. They will not simply let us be. In
one way or another they are always on our backs,
forever admonishing us that there is no such thing as
life apart from relationship, which is to say, no life
apart from the sharing of ourselves with another.[4]
Mike Mason

Insight into my wife

5. a. How would my wife describe her role as a companion and helper to me? *not always but at times she encourages me*

b. Does my wife feel that she is an important part of my life as my "corresponding partner"? Why or why not?

because she has a hard time grasping, and memorizes scripture. She feels enfour and underestimates her worth.

And where better to view the truth of my self than in one who neither flatters nor scorns me, but knows me well and lovingly?

This mirroring is a most practical "help" to all my work, for I will be wise to my strengths and watchful of my weaknesses thereafter. Neither falsely proud nor falsely inferior, I can make realistic, efficient decisions.[5]

Walter Wangerin, Jr.

Insight from an older man

Sometimes this beautiful woman I courted and felt that I couldn't live without seems to become more of a hindrance and an interruption than a help. In my selfishness it just seems easier not to have my "helper" around!

But the problem is not, of course, my wife—my argument is with God, who gave her to me. Remember Adam's plea when things weren't going well in the garden of Eden? "It is this woman You gave me!" I need to have a right view of God and of the woman who is to be my completer, my crown—for God loves me and gives me every good and perfect gift.

As I acknowledge God's gift to me I also should seek to enhance my wife's ability to be a helper. For me personally, that means considering Cynthia a source of encouragement and competent counsel.

[My wife] was not designed to be my echo, a little vanilla shadow curled up in a corner awaiting my next order. She was designed by God to be my counterpart, a necessary and needed individual to help me become all God wanted me to be.[6]

Charles R. Swindoll

Suggested Scripture memory: Proverbs 18:22

NOTES
1. Matthew Henry, *Commentary on the Whole Bible,* vol. I (Iowa Falls: Riverside Book & Bible House, n.d.), page 20.
2. Mike Mason, *The Mystery of Marriage* (Portland, Oreg.: Multnomah Press, 1985), page 47.
3. Charles R. Swindoll, *Strike the Original Match* (Portland, Oreg.: Multnomah Press, 1980), page 19.
4. Mason, pages 42-43.
5. Walter Wangerin, Jr., *As for Me and My House: Crafting Your Marriage to Last* (Nashville: Thomas Nelson Publishers, 1987), page 61.
6. Swindoll, page 20.

"Live with Your Wives in an Understanding Way"

Be good husbands to your wives.
Honor them, delight in them.
As women they lack some of your
advantages. But in the new life of
God's grace, you're equals.
Treat your wives, then, as equals so
your prayers don't run aground.
1 Peter 3:7 (Message)

The essential foundation for a biblical
marriage relationship is an
unqualified commitment to the goal
of ministry. Each partner must be
willing to minister to the needs of the
other regardless of the response.
Although all of us will fail to implement
that commitment perfectly, our
responsibility is to remind ourselves
continually that our highest purpose
as husbands or wives is to be an
instrument for promoting our partners'
spiritual and personal welfare.[1]
Lawrence J. Crabb, Jr.

Husbands & wifes have Diffrent God-given Roles They need to work Together in fulfilling them

LESSON 4

In medieval new year's festivities the couple who had lived the most harmoniously during the previous year was awarded a slab of pork. This is the origin of the phrase "bringing home the bacon"! Harmony, especially in the home, requires both husband and wife working together, fulfilling their God-given roles. A husband's understanding and consideration of his "special vessel" is commanded by God as a requirement for answered prayer and evidence to others of his discipleship at home.

Insight into Scripture

1. Included in the law that Moses passed on to the Israelites is one interesting passage concerning the newly married.

    Read Deuteronomy 24:5 and write down your thoughts about what this verse means and why it is included in the Scriptures. *God saw that sepration from a new wife was not good for the marrage. They would need time to get to know each other. A couple Don't get to know each other by seeing each other once in awhile.*

2. a. The word *deacon* means "minister" or "servant." Paul instructs Timothy on the necessary qualifications for men who want to serve or minister. Read 1 Timothy 3:8-10, 12-13 and write down these qualifications.

    1. must be reverent. 2. Not Doubled — Tongued. 3. Not Greed for money. 4. Strong in the Faith. 5. Have only one wife and to Train His Children and rule their Household well—

b. How can the qualities taught in these verses help husbands to live with their wives in an understanding way? *If I have the qualifications as a deacon Than these will help me live with my wife in an understanding way.*

---

3. In 1 Peter 3:7, Peter says a lot to husbands in just one verse. In order to understand this verse in its context, answer the questions below.

a. Summarize 1 Peter 2:11–3:6. *Abstain from fleshly Lust — answer have no part of sexual activity with any one else other than the one you are married to. Lust wars against the Soul. 3:6 Discuss*

b. Now read 1 Peter 3:7 along with 3:1. What does "in the same way" or "likewise" refer to? *Like as Jesus was obedient. So likewise are we to be as Jesus was*

c. Define what is meant by living in an "understanding" or "considerate" way. *we are to be considerate of who our wife is treat Her tenderhearted and be Courteous.*

d. In what sense is the wife the weaker "partner" or "vessel"? *my wife in many ways Dosesent Have the same strength that I have some thing She does better than me other things I Do better than Her.*

e. How can a husband bestow honor on, or treat with respect, his wife? *when we are out together I can treat Her as a lady, be Kind and show Her respect. pint Put your wife Down in front of others*

39

f. What is the consequence of a husband's failure to
   honor or respect his wife, and why do you think
   Peter mentions this consequence?

Our prayers may be Hindered

g. Summarize 1 Peter 3:8-12. *be of one mind,
have compassion, love as Brothers,
be tenderhearted and courteous.
not evil for evil or reviling. we are to turn
from sinful pleasures, 3:12 shows us how. the
eyes of God are on the righteous His Blessings are
on*

h. How does all of 1 Peter 2:11-3:12 relate to and help
   interpret 1 Peter 3:7? *2:11 Helps us see us
who we are and that we are Travelers
passing Through This life*

i. What have you learned from this analysis of 1 Peter
   3:7 that will help you in being a more considerate
   husband? *That my wife and I are
Heirs together in the grace of
God. if I want my prayers ans.*

The setting for all role relationships is that we all
belong to, need, and must submit to one another as
joint-heirs of the grace of life. Even in exercising his
function as leader of others in the church, an elder or
bishop must serve others. Even in exercising his
headship over his wife, the husband must submit to
and honor her as a joint-heir of the grace of life, an
equal by both creation and redemption.[2]
                    George W. Knight, III

40

Insight into myself

4. a. What qualities of a deacon do I exemplify?
   One wife only & try to all ways be honest in my Dealings with others, when our Children were growing up & Teamed from The ways of Jesus

   b. What qualities do I need to work on? *I need to pay more attention to things She is talking about,*

   c. In what ways do I show honor to, or treat with respect, my wife? *by Helping Her around the House as to by includeing Her in things I do.*

> God's Word warns us against *demanding instead of managing*. The male—especially the insecure male—tends to use force and intimidation, demanding certain things of his wife. The verse [1 Peter 3:7] clearly states that of the two, the wife is the weaker partner. She is like a delicate vessel, deeply in need of being understood. Rare is the husband who spends time and thought coming to an understanding of his wife's needs so he can provide wise management as the leader of his home. Biblical management. Wholesome, positive, helpful management.[3]
> Charles R. Swindoll

Insight into my wife

5. a. Would my wife say that I am considerate of her? Why or why not? *yes*

b. What are some things I know my wife would like me to do with her and for her?

with her To SHOP with her She wants me To know her needs FOR her Suprise her with Special Gifts

c. Does my wife feel that I honor her (or show her respect) publicly and in our home? Why or why not?

yes — yes

Insight from an older man

Some days it seems easier to be involved in the corporate wars, exciting ministry, sports events, pet projects, and other "important" things than it is to give my wife a call and tell her I will be late for supper. Before we were married, however, I certainly took advantage of every opportunity to be with her, to consider her, to be available if she needed me.

I believe that the "weaker vessel" refers to God's creation of my wife for a special place in my life. Since she has voluntarily agreed to follow my leadership, I need to be a good steward of this special partner. God has asked me to give Cynthia honor. Just as people see that I take special care of rare and delicate things in our home, such as crystal glasses or family heirlooms, so I must give special care to my wife, who has been given to me for special use. I can learn to listen to Cynthia, to know what pleases her, to laugh with her. When she is upset and I don't understand, I can admit not knowing how to help. It has really helped both of us for me to learn to say, "I don't understand what the problem is, but I *want* to understand"—and mean it. It sure isn't easy—but men, I want to "bring home the bacon" for a lot of years. I want to live in an "understanding way" so we can enjoy being heirs together of the grace of life.

42

Note

Peter is commanding us to be experts about our wives. Most successful husbands I know make it a point to ask their wives about their emotional, spiritual, physical, and intellectual needs. . . . Do you know what a perfect day is for your wife? A perfect date? What she *really* likes to do on vacations? If not, you'd better find out! Peter commands us to know our wives and to allow them access to us, or he warns that sin and struggle will reign and our prayers will not be answered. How can we be out of fellowship with our wives and expect God to answer when we call?[4]

Don Meredith

Suggested Scripture memory: 1 Peter 3:7

NOTES
1. Lawrence J. Crabb, Jr., *The Marriage Builder* (Grand Rapids: Zondervan Publishing House, 1982), page 63.
2. George W. Knight, III, *The New Testament Teaching on the Role Relationship of Men and Women* (Grand Rapids: Baker Book House, 1977), page 59.
3. Charles R. Swindoll, *Strike the Original Match* (Portland, Oreg.: Multnomah Press, 1980), page 63.
4. Don Meredith, *Becoming One* (Nashville: Thomas Nelson Publishers, n.d.), pages 134-135.

"Husbands, Love Your Wives, Just as Christ Loved the Church"

*By no means do I count myself an expert in
all of this, but I've got my eye on the goal,
where God is beckoning us onward—
to Jesus. I'm off and running,
and I'm not turning back.*

*So let's keep focused on that goal, those of us
who want everything God has for us.
If any of you have something else in mind,
something less than total commitment, God
will clear your blurred vision—you'll see it yet!
Now that we're on the right track,
let's stay on it.*
Philippians 3:12-16 (MESSAGE)

*Our ultimate goal, our highest calling in life,
is to glorify God—not to be happy. Let that
sink in! Glorifying Him is our greatest pursuit.
Not to get our way. Not to be comfortable.
Not to find fulfillment. Not even to be loved,
or to be appreciated or to be taken care of.
Now these are important, but they
are not primary.*

*As I glorify Him, He sees to it that other
essential needs are met . . . or my need
for them diminishes. Believe me, this concept
will change your entire perspective on yourself,
your life, and your marriage.*[1]
Charles R. Swindoll

45

| LESSON 5 | "Love so amazing, so divine . . ." is how the hymn writer describes the love God has for us. The divine part of God's love is that He loves me even though I don't deserve it. God teaches me by His |

Spirit who He is, how amazing His sacrificial love is for me, and how He wants to demonstrate His resurrection power in me to my wife. To love Cynthia as Christ loves the Church will "demand my life, my all."

Insight into Scripture

1. "The word 'love' (*agapáo*) means seeking the highest good for another person. This is an unselfish love as seen in Christ's sacrificial death in which He gave Himself up for the church."[2] If we, as husbands, are to love as Christ loved the Church, then we must consider Christ's example and His teaching.

   Read Philippians 2:5-16 and answer the following questions.

   a. Define "attitude." *State of mind or feeling*

   b. What attitude did Christ have? *Servent Hood He came to give*

   c. How did Christ exemplify this attitude? *by taking our place on the Cross*

   d. How does this entire passage encourage you to love your wife sacrificially? *Having the mind of christ Helps me, seeing what Christ Did also Helps me, Knowing that God is working in me Helps me.*

46

2. Read John 15:12-14 and write down Jesus' description of love. *Love makes us love others, Love causes us to lay down our lives for others love will cause us to do what Christ Commands.*

3. Understanding the source of our love for others is important. Read 1 John 4:7-21.

   a. Write down the key observations given about love in this passage. *Love is of God Love shows that we are Borned of God God showed his love for us by sending His only son in to the world. not to love is not to know God.*

   b. What are the basic truths in these verses that can also apply to the marriage relationship?
   each other is to love the other

4. There are scriptural examples of husbands who loved sacrificially. Read the verses below and comment on how Hosea and Joseph loved their wives.

   Hosea 3:1-3 *Hosea was willing to pay for a wife who was unfaithful to him, and after bringing her in to his House, He said He would be*

47

a man to Her.

Matthew 1:18-25 *Joseph loved Mary the mother of Jesus so much, He did not want make a public show of Her, He was going to Hide Her till all this passed.*

The electing love of God is also in the background of Eph. 5:22ff., where the relationship between man and wife is compared with the love of Christ for the church. There are two points of contact here. On the one hand, there is the election of Israel (cf. Rom. 9); the church is the called-out body, the new Israel which has come to faith in Christ. On the other hand, there is the OT picture of marriage dating from the time of Hosea with the implication of a relationship of fidelity and covenant love. What is true for the Christian community is true also for the individual, and is also true for marriage. God's love is able to overcome every kind of difficulty and infidelity. Electing love is at the same time compassionate and forgiving love.[3]

Insight into myself

5. a. What attitude do I generally exemplify in my marriage? *I am not always unselfish*

b. What are some ways I lay down my life for my wife?
Thinking of Her instead of myself.

c. What is my greatest hindrance to loving my wife sacrificially? *Self.*

The willingness to give unconditionally does not come by simply deciding to be selfless. The stain of self-centeredness requires many washings before it no longer controls our motivation. Many commitments to minister and much time spent with God will transpire before we know what it means to *give.* Our job is to learn faithfulness and to press on in obedience, not giving in to discouragement or weariness, believing that God will always honor the conscious and persevering motivation to serve Him. When a spouse becomes more critical, drinks more heavily, or rejects efforts of ministry, we are to continue in our obedience, believing that our responsibility before God is to obey and to trust Him for the outcome.[4]

Lawrence J. Crabb, Jr.

Insight into my wife

6. a. How would my wife describe my attitude toward her? *Good & Bad* .

b. Is my wife secure in the knowledge that I seek her highest good? Why or why not? *yes, because she has Trust in me*

If human love does not carry a man beyond himself, it is not love. If love is always discreet, always wise, always sensible and calculating, never carried beyond itself, it is not love at all. It may be affection, it may be warmth of feeling, but it has not the true nature of love in it.[5]

Oswald Chambers

Insight from an older man

Obedience to God's command! To think of myself willingly and unselfishly doing *anything* God asks is amazing—and would certainly surprise Cynthia. But God has not asked me to do anything He hasn't given me the ability to do. He has provided His Spirit, the Scriptures, and the encouragement of godly people to accomplish in me what He has commanded.

I am to love my wife as Christ loves the Church; this fact remains however circumstances, feelings, and thoughts may change. Commitment in the bond of marriage is the basis for love; love is not the basis of marriage. Only God can love first!

A great misconception of marriage circulating today is the idea of fifty/fifty partnership. I must give 110 percent *regardless* of my wife's response. But this does not come naturally to me. I don't like being a servant, and I respond rather poorly when I'm treated like one. Years ago a friend asked me about my routine when arriving home in the evening from work. I described how I liked "my space," a newspaper, and uninterrupted watching of the six o'clock news—all of this in the context of four children and dinner activities! My friend asked me to consider whether I should come home to serve or to be served. Of course I had lots of rationalizations for my performance, but none held up to the test of Scripture and Christ's example.

I want my life and my message at home to read like Paul's: "For we do not preach ourselves but Christ Jesus as Lord and ourselves as your bondservants for Jesus' sake" (2 Corinthians 4:5).

Christ serves the church and the church serves Christ, just as there is mutual service between husband and wife. Yet, Christ's authority over the church is in no way undermined by his self-giving love.[6]
                    Susan T. Foh

Suggested Scripture memory: 1 John 4:15-16

NOTES
1. Charles R. Swindoll, *Strike the Original Match* (Portland, Oreg.: Multnomah Press, 1980), page 41.
2. From *The Bible Knowledge Commentary,* edited by John F. Walvoord & Roy B. Zuck (Wheaton: Victor Books, 1983), page 641.
3. W. Gunther & H. G. Link, in *The New International Dictionary of New Testament Theology,* edited by Colin Brown, vol. 2 (Grand Rapids: Zondervan, 1971), page 545.
4. Lawrence J. Crabb, Jr., *The Marriage Builder* (Grand Rapids: Zondervan Publishing House, 1982), pages 58-59.
5. Oswald Chambers, *My Utmost for His Highest* (New York: Dodd, Mead & Company, 1966), page 52.
6. Susan T. Foh, *Women and the Word of God: A Response to Biblical Feminism* (Phillipsburg, N.J.: Presbyterian and Reformed Publishing Co., 1979), page 200.

"Husbands Ought to Love Their Wives as Their Own Bodies"

So husbands ought also to love their own wives as their own bodies. He who loves his own wife loves himself; for no one ever hated his own flesh, but nourishes and cherishes it, just as Christ also does the church, because we are members of His body.

Ephesians 5:28-30

Next to the love of God, the "one thing" that is by far the most important in the life of all married people is their marriage, their loving devotion to their partner. Nothing on earth must take precedence over that, not children, jobs, other friendships, nor even "Christian work."[1]

Mike Mason

The Bible presupposes that we love ourselves because of our sin nature. But because of our new nature in Christ, we are empowered to love unselfishly. We can now "not merely look out for [our] own personal interests, but also for the interests of others" (Philippians 2:4). Because of Christ's provision for my needs, I can love my wife, I can learn to nourish and cherish her—for Christ loves, nourishes, and cherishes me.

Insight into Scripture

1. a. The following verses exhort us to love. Read these scriptures and write down the key thought of each passage.

Matthew 22:34-40 *greed wanting what belonged to another.*

John 13:34 *love one another*

Galatians 5:22-23 *The Fruit of the Spirit is Love, Joy, PEACE, LongsuFFering, KindNess, goodNess, FAITHFulNess, GentLNess, SelF CONTRoll.*

1 Thessalonians 4:9-10 *we are taught love by God, and are urged to love more and increase more + more in love.*

1 Peter 1:22 *Love one another fervently with a pure Heart.*

b. How do these verses encourage you to love your wife?. *with out selfiness*

2. remember the golden rull: .
3. alow the Fruit of the spirit. to work in us. 4. as we increase in love we will love our wife more

54

2. Any study on love must consider 1 Corinthians 13:1-7. The Greek word used in these verses is *agape*, which expresses unselfish esteem for the object loved, not just mutual affection.[2] Study Paul's description of love and write down how each of the aspects of love can guide you specifically in deepening your love and friendship with your wife.

1. with out love, sounding Brass or a Clinging Cymbal
2. if I have Gift of prophecy, Know all mysties, have all faith so I can move mountains, with out love I am nothing.
3. feed the poor, give my to be burned, w.O.L. NO PROFIT To me.
4.5.6.7. Suffers Longs, is Kind, Not envyous, seeks not its own Rejoices not in iniquity, hears all thing, endures all things

3. Paul instructs husbands to love their wives with a most practical comparison—to love them as they love their own bodies. Read Ephesians 5:28-30 and answer the following questions.

a. In what ways do you love your body? nourishes and cherishes it.

b. Why do you think Paul wrote, "He who loves his own wife loves himself"? because God says we are one body

c. How can you nourish and cherish your wife?

encourage Her in the things of God though the word.

55

4. a. Elkanah and the husband of the Proverbs 31 wife
illustrate how husbands can nourish and cherish
their wives. Read the passages below and record how
these husbands loved their wives.

1 Samuel 1:1-8 *Am I not better to you*
than ten sons

Proverbs 31:11,28-29 *Her Husband trust Her*
Her children call Her Blessed
He Toled Her out of many Daughters, she
exceled
b. Contrast these passages to Genesis 12:10-20. After *them*
reading it, write a few sentences telling why you *all*
think Abraham did what he did and what you think
of his decision.

Abram was afraid He would be Killed
As He dident want Sarah to be
with out a Husband He ask his
wife to Say she was his Sister There
was some truth in this. They Both were
spared.

5. Ephesians 3:14-19 is a beautiful prayer concerning
being rooted and grounded in love. Read these verses
and write down the main petitions. Pray this prayer for
yourself as a husband. (You might also pray this prayer
for your wife.)

bow Knees to the Father of our Lord
Jesus Christ. to be strengthened through
His Spirit in the inner man, that Christ may
dwell in our Hearts through Faith. Rooted
and grounded in love what is
the with and length and depth and height—
To Know The love of 56 *Christ which passes*
all
Knowledge he filled the fulloops of God

And so the best marriages and the deepest relationships with God grow out of the startling discovery
that there is nothing one can do to earn love, and
even more startling, that there is also nothing one can
do to un-earn it, or to keep onself from being loved.
This is a religious awakening that is utterly different
from any other religious experience, no matter how
profoundly spiritual it may seem. It is the recognition
of the true self in the simple discovery that one is
loved. "How beautiful you are, my darling! Oh, how
beautiful!" say the words of the fourth chapter of the
Song of Songs. "You have stolen my heart with one
glance of your eyes." They are the words of God Himself speaking personally, with outrageous intimacy, to
every human soul.[3]

Mike Mason

Insight into myself

6. a. How do I know that God loves me? *John 3:16*
Jesus said no one Takes my life I lay it down
Jesus said come unto me, God Gave us power to
become sons of God.

   b. In what ways do I draw upon the love of God in
   order to love as I should? *I Tottaly look to the*
   word of God for ways He loved so I
   Can do the same.

   c. Do I consider my wife a good friend? Why? *Yes*
   because we Have so many things in Common
   our years together our Family our church

   d. Do I understand my wife's feelings and what her *Family*
   needs are? Why or why not?

   most of the time even tho I dont have
   the means to do as I would like
   most of the time 57 *Her need are simple*
   and she might Just need my Time.

e. In what ways do I communicate love and friendship
to my wife?

1. Stand by Her, Support Her, love Her as Christ also loves each of us
2. We share with each other She is my Best Friend

f. How is my love for my wife evident to other people?

People can See, Just as you can see and know fruit so you can see it between to people

g. From studying 1 Corinthians 13 what is my greatest
area of need in loving my wife?

my greatest need I think is my sometimes not treating Her as an equal.

h. What can I begin to do to deepen my love for my
wife?

I need to get closer my self to the Lord and as His love fills my life, I will begain to be different and Show more love to Her.

The knowledge that God has loved me to the utter-
most, to the end of all my sin and meanness and selfishness and wrong, will send me forth into the world
to love in the same way. God's love to me is inex-
haustible, and I must love others from the bedrock of
God's love to me. Growth in grace stops the moment
I get huffed. I get huffed because I have a peculiar
person to live with. Just think how disagreeable I
have been to God! Am I prepared to be so identified
with the Lord Jesus that His life and His sweetness are
being poured out all the time? Neither natural love
nor Divine love will remain unless it is cultivated.
Love is spontaneous, but it has to be maintained by
discipline.[4]

Oswald Chambers

Insight into my wife

7. a. How would my wife define love? *My wife thinks of love in Terms of wine & Roses How my husband show me affection.*

b. Does my wife consider me a good friend? Why?

yes at Times, and other time no why its how she feels at the time.

c. How would my wife respond if I asked her, "What is one thing I do that hurts you?" *she would say I am at times inconsiterate of Her, when I forget about Her*

d. In what way would my wife like me "to excel still more" in my love for her?

in the ways of the statements above -

The apostle Paul didn't say that love bears some things, that love believes only in the best things, that love hopes for a reasonable period of time, or that it endures for a while. No, love is a divine absurdity. It is unreasonable. Paul said, "Love bears *all* things, believes *all* things, hopes *all* things, endures *all* things." Love is limit*less.* For-give-ness is to give infinitely, without end.[5]

Walter Wangerin, Jr.

Insight from an older man

The story goes that a man told his counselor, "Sure I love my wife. I told her that when we got married ten years ago.

If I change my mind, I'll let her know!" You can see why they were in the counselor's office!

How often do I tell my wife that I love her? How much time do I spend with her? How much time do I spend on personal grooming and physical conditioning? If I looked at my weekly schedule, how would my wife rate in importance next to all my activities? Do I love her as much as I love myself?

The most effective ministry I have is my marriage and family, although I don't deserve the credit. Look around you to see what discredits a testimony more than a ruined marriage. Most of the activity of Satan and the world system around us is working overtime to destroy the most important human relationship. I can either decide to regard my wife in a manner honoring God, or I can "punt" the whole issue. I know what I want to do—do you?

Some things that have helped me in loving Cynthia as myself are: (1) have my own time with the Lord and His Word each day; (2) pray with Cynthia daily; (3) have a "date" time each week of at least two hours; (4) ask her frequently if she feels that I have listened to and understood how she is feeling about us, the family, and life in general.

Do yourself a favor—love your wife!

The husband's chief duty is to love his wife as Christ loved the church. The most common description of Christ's love in this context is "self-sacrificing." Christ's love for the church is self-sacrificing with a purpose—to sanctify and to present her to himself in splendor, without blemish. And so the husband is to nourish and cherish his wife. He is to do for his wife what he would do for himself. He is to encourage her growth into the image of Christ and to help her develop and use her gifts. But how does one do that? Christ knows his bride's needs and how to meet them; he knows what her goal is and how to reach it.[6]
Susan T. Foh

Suggested Scripture memory: 1 Peter 1:22

NOTES
1. Mike Mason, *The Mystery of Marriage* (Portland, Oreg.: Multnomah Press, 1985), page 99.
2. From a reference note on 1 Corinthians 13:1 in *The Ryrie Study Bible: New American Standard Translation,* edited by Charles Caldwell Ryrie (Chicago: Moody Press, 1978), page 1744.
3. Mason, pages 63-64.
4. Oswald Chambers, *My Utmost for His Highest* (New York: Dodd, Mead & Company, 1966), page 132.
5. Walter Wangerin, Jr., *As for Me and My House: Crafting Your Marriage to Last* (Nashville: Thomas Nelson Publishers, 1987), page 81.
6. Susan T. Foh, *Women and the Word of God: A Response to Biblical Feminism* (Phillipsburg, N.J.: Presbyterian and Reformed Publishing Co., 1979), pages 201-202.

"For the Husband Is the Head of the Wife"

For the husband is the head of the wife, as Christ also is the head of the church, He Himself being the Savior of the body.

Ephesians 5:23

Headship and lordship of Christ does not consist in authoritarianism. Rather, it is expressed precisely in self-giving. For Paul, Christ's lordship was exercised precisely in taking the form of a servant. Likewise, the husband's headship is to be exercised in the same self-giving in which he lives out his new nature in Christ. The headship consists in a renunciation of all authoritarianism; the only subjection that it is to demand is self-subjection for love of the wife.[1]

Colin Brown

<table>
<tr><td>LESSON
7</td><td>Christ's attitude and example of becoming a serv-
ant and not using His ultimate authority over us is
amazing leadership. We are told to be the head of
our wife according to the example of Christ's head-</td></tr>
</table>

ship of the church. It is His plan and pattern that gives us
the opportunity to prove His good and perfect will without
being conformed to the world's model of marriage. To
lead my wife as Christ leads the church can only take place
in the context of self-giving.

Insight into Scripture

1. Eve, tempted by Satan, yielded to sin and then influ-
enced her husband to do the same. What can we learn
from this original seduction to help us today? Read
Genesis 3:1-19 and answer the following questions.

a. Why do you think Satan approached Eve and not
Adam? *because Eve dident have the same revelation that Her husband*

b. In what areas was Eve particularly vulnerable?
She was limited in Her knowledge of what God had said She was not there when God first spoke to adam.

c. How did Adam respond concerning his sin?

adam blamed the woman that God had given Him

d. How did God respond to Adam?
God said to adam because you have done what your wife told you rather than to listen me you are going to have to work the ground cursed

2. When God spoke to Eve after the Fall, He said, "Yet
your desire shall be for your husband, and he shall rule
over you" (Genesis 3:16). Susan Foh interprets this
pronouncement, "The 'curse' here describes the
beginning of the battle of the sexes. After the fall, the

husband no longer rules easily, he must fight for his headship. The woman's desire is to control her husband (to usurp his divinely appointed headship), and he must master her, if he can. Sin has corrupted both the willing submission of the wife and loving headship of the husband. And so, the rule of love founded in paradise is replaced by struggle, tyranny, domination, and manipulation."[2]

a. How do you see this interpretation exemplified in marriages today? where Two parents are trying to both be in Head Ship their children can see what is Happening real fast so they take advantge of this fast there are many more ways.

b. How do these thoughts help you in understanding your relationship to your wife? I realize how Satan has Corrupted both man & woman so they Can not act in love any more. I need to have a loving head ship of my Fam.

3. a. Scripture records conversations and actions of husbands and wives. Read the verses below and summarize the events recorded. The wife sarah took matters

Genesis 16:1-5 into her own hands by telling abram to sleep with her hand maid so she could have a child she didn't he god. abram listened and did as she said. the results was a mess.

Genesis 21:1-7 in these verses some time later God did as He had promised abram. but by this time it was to late to undo the thing she had done which was out of God's will for them. the son which she tried to get her own way became an outcast to her. she threw her maid and son out of her house.

b. Write down your thoughts about how Abraham
   handled his role as head in his marriage.

Abram lost his Head ship over his house after He followed her advice He continued to do what she ask.

---

4. Paul instructs the Corinthians concerning headship and
   the relationship between men and women. Read
   1 Corinthians 11:2-16. What do you think Paul is teach-
   ing in verses 3, 8-9, and 11-12? *The Head of man is christ, the Head of woman is man, and the Head of christ is God. Man is not from woman but the other way around. Neither man or woman are Independent of each other*

---

5. Ephesians 5:23 states that the husband is the head of
   his wife as Christ is the head of the Church. List ways in
   which Christ exercises His headship of the Church that
   are appropriate models for the husband's exercise of
   his headship in the family. *Christ had a Servent spirit, He also said He was laying down His life for His Sheep - (DISCIPLES) and the church.*

The headship of God in reference to Christ can be
readily seen and affirmed with no threat to Christ's
identity. This chain of subordination with its implica-
tions is apparently given to help answer the objection
some bring to the headship of man in reference to
woman. Just as Christ is not a second-class person or
deity because the Father is His head, so the woman is
not a second-class person or human being because
man is her head.[3]

George W. Knight III

Insight into myself

6. a. How would I define my role as head of my home? *Provide for my family, I want the good for all in my home, to worship, instruct and teach the word to take the lead in serving the Lord.*

b. What problems, if any, do I have in exercising my role of headship in my marriage? *none*

c. In what ways is a servant attitude present or absent in my leadership style? *Through serving others thinking of others first*

d. What are some improvements I can make in my leadership of my home? *I can only make improvements in my home, as I seek the master of all.*

It is absolutely imperative, men, that we fight our tendency to be passive in matters pertaining to the home. The passive husband continues to be one of the most common complaints I hear from troubled homes. Men, *get with it!* Your wife will grow in her respect for you as soon as she sees your desire to take the leadership and management of the home.[4]

Charles R. Swindoll *amen*

Insight into my wife

7. a. Does my wife consider me a servant/leader in our
home? Why or why not? *I believe so*

b. How does my servant/leadership contribute to my
wife's sense of being loved in our relationship?

*She knows the way I treat Her
that I respect Her, she sences
love in our relationship.
I alway want Her best intrest*

c. How does my servant/leadership contribute to my
wife's security in submitting to me?

*She shows me that she is
secure in submitting to me
in Her trust in me. as I lead.*

> Problems with the hierarchical model for marriage
> arise only when husband and/or wife are disobeying
> God's Word. The husband is commanded to nourish
> and cherish his wife, and so his decisions should be
> qualified by concern for his wife's best interests.
> When the husband obeys God's commands, the wife
> suffers no hardship through her submission to him.[5]
> Susan T. Foh

Insight from an older man

When I was growing up, a humorous—but all too
serious— view of marriage in my part of the country was
that a husband should keep his wife "barefoot and preg-

nant." Perhaps this sentiment was popular because it did not require of the husband any real commitment to the marriage.

Commitment, of course, is crucial, but so is the way in which we carry it out. There are three common ways men exert leadership in the home. The first is *domineering authoritarianism*. A man with this pattern will rarely let his wife make any independent decision, basically because he doesn't trust her—he doesn't see her as capable of fulfilling her God-given role. This man ignores the fact that God gave him a good gift and thereby offends God and deprives himself of the companionship and help of a friend and lover.

A second leadership style is actually a lack of leadership; men with this pattern are *passively indifferent*. They become absorbed in their own activities and avoid involvement with home or family. These men are fearful of making decisions at home even though they make major decisions at work. They tell their wife, "whatever you want to do, honey," but then are quick to turn around and criticize her or hold on to suppressed, negative feelings about her decisions.

A third way of exercising leadership is to follow *Christ's example of headship*. The husband who seeks to conform to this pattern will share with his wife the authority of their family while retaining his sense of responsibility for her and their home. He will remember that she is his equal in creation and redemption and therefore worthy of his trust.

If I am to be head of my wife as Christ is head of the church, I will need not only total commitment to my marriage but also love, wisdom, sacrifice, and submission to *my* Lord.

Let this same attitude and purpose and [humble] mind be in you which was in Christ Jesus.—Let Him be your example in humility."
Philippians 2:5 (AMP)

Suggested Scripture memory: Ephesians 5:23

NOTES
1. Colin Brown, in *The New International Dictionary of New Testament Theology,* edited by Colin Brown, vol. 3 (Grand Rapids: Zondervan, 1971), page 1064.
2. Susan T. Foh, *Women and the Word of God: A Response to Biblical Feminism* (Phillipsburg, N.J.: Presbyterian and Reformed Publishing Co., 1979), page 69.
3. George W. Knight, III, *The New Testament Teaching on the Role Relationship of Men and Women* (Grand Rapids: Baker Book House, 1977), page 33.
4. Charles R. Swindoll, *Strike the Original Match* (Portland, Oreg.: Multnomah Press, 1980), page 51.
5. Foh, page 200.

"Husbands, Love Your Wives, and Do Not Be Embittered"

Husbands, love your wives—be affectionate and sympathetic with them—and do not be harsh or bitter or resentful toward them.
Colossians 3:19 (AMP)

All of us face various character-molding decisions every day. To speak with my spouse, I must consciously and deliberately think: "My purpose right now must be to help my wife realize her value as a person. What can I do that will accomplish this?" My insides may urgently scream with a compelling desire to defend myself, criticize her, or make other manipulative responses. Amid this inner turmoil, I must make a decision to do what will help her feel loved. As I make the choice, the Spirit of God provides the power to make it real— but I must make the choice.[1]
Lawrence J. Crabb, Jr.

"You only hurt the one you love" was a popular song years ago. Pop music often reflects life's realities. How easy it is to hurt those we love—and to think that they simply have to accept our "justified" anger, our careless attitudes, our hurtful behavior. Becoming hardened and bitter is something we husbands need to guard against, and we have a direct command against it from God's Word to drive home how susceptible we are to this destructive tendency.

Insight into Scripture

---

1. Using a dictionary or thesaurus, define the words below. If possible, record several synonyms for each word.

   bitter— *Biter, Akin To Bite, unPleasant Taste. Sharp, and disagreeable; Harsh. Resentful, or cynical.*

   embittered— *To make Bitter*

   strife— *#1 Contention, #2 Fighting or ~~struggle~~, quarreling: struggle.*

   anger— *distress) a feeling of displeasure and hostility a person has been injured, mistreated, opposed, etc become angry.*

---

2. a. The Lord knows our hearts, and His Word accurately diagnoses our problems. What reasons for contention and strife are given in the following verses?

   Proverbs 10:12

Proverbs 13:10 *Pride*

Proverbs 15:4 ~~Pow~~ *Perverseness*

Proverbs 15:18 *Wrathful*

Proverbs 20:3 *Fool.*

Proverbs 28:25 *Proud Heart.*

James 4:1-3 *your desires, Lust, covet, we do not ask. when we do we ask amiss.*

b. What impressed you most about the causes of strife?

Its so much About Self.

---

3. Scripture also instructs us positively "in the way we should go." What do the verses below teach us about overcoming bitterness and anger?

Proverbs 10:12 *To Love*

Proverbs 15:4 *Be carful of what we speak or say.*

Proverbs 16:7 *Keep a close check on the way we live.*

Proverbs 16:21 *Keep filled with the Holy Spirit so we can have a wise Heart.*

73

Proverbs 19:11 *DISCRETION..*
the freedom to make ~~decisions~~
decisions
Ephesians 4:26-27 *be angry sin not*
give no place to the devil.

---

4. a. Bitterness can be devastating not only to individuals, but also to families. What admonition concerning bitterness is given in Hebrews 12:14-15?

go after peace
don't fall short of Gods Grace

b. What are the results of letting bitterness take root?

it causes Trouble and many will become defiled

c. Who do you think the "many" in this passage might be? *it could be our partner or family members or people we work with.*

d. What do you think can be done to keep bitterness from taking root?

Keep filled with the word and the Holy Spirit.

One of the most devastating things that can occur in marriage is for the husband to become critical toward his wife, to treat her with scorn, or to be sarcastic toward her. This is one of the important causes of disintegration in marriage, for such an attitude threatens the basic nature of woman. As Lord Byron put it, "Man's love is of man's life a thing apart. 'Tis woman's whole existence." It is the man's job, therefore, to make his wife feel important to him and never to let his love decay into taking her for granted.[2]

Raymond C. Stedman

5. a. When I am contentious, what prompts or motivates me to be quarrelsome? *when tired and stressed.*

   b. What do I feel? *(Egitable) I need my wife to understand me.*

   c. What do I want? *↙*

   d. Is what I want consistent with what God wants for me? Explain. *no. God wants me to have a quite spirit, so I can see things different.*

   e. As a Christian, what are my choices? *to seek the Lord pray and read the word. and let the Lord know how I feel*

6. Am I content with my wife? Have I accepted her for just who she is—imperfections and all? Why or why not? *yes I do accept her for who she is most of the time, I wish it was all the time.*

7. When David was contentious and angry because some-one had caused him great strife and hurt, he wrote down his feelings to God (Psalm 55 and Psalm 109 are good examples). When we feel bitter and need to complain and murmur, where are we to go? The Lord wants us to come before Him in honesty, telling Him

75

everything. This must be done frequently.

In taking our complaints to God, we gain release, perspective, and strength—and we'll also find out it's a good antidote to bitterness.

Perhaps with pen in hand you can take time now to "pour out your heart to God." He knows your thoughts, but it is important that you acknowledge them to Him.

> The refusal to be disillusioned is the cause of much of the suffering in human life. It works in this way—if we love a human being and do not love God, we demand of him every perfection and every rectitude, and when we do not get it we become cruel and vindictive; we are demanding of a human being that which he or she cannot give. There is only one Being Who can satisfy the last aching abyss of the human heart, and that is the Lord Jesus Christ.[3]
> Oswald Chambers

Insight into my wife

8. a. In what area would my wife say I am most likely to be bitter and quarrelsome?

   b. How does my wife respond to my contentiousness?

c. Would my wife say that I am content with her? Why or why not?

---

9. What steps can I take to guard against bitterness?

The New Testament Scripture with the passage quoted by Peter from Psalm 34:13-17 is very plain. God has called every Christian into a lifestyle of consistent blessing of others through (1) *words;* (2) *behavior.* This means consistently blessing those in our own household—our marriage partner first of all. Blessing in word and action is most especially required of us in response to any manner of evil behavior or insulting speech. As you apply this to your own marriage, understand that you never have any justification for speaking to your partner scornfully, angrily, or deceitfully. Your partner's bad behavior can never excuse your own in God's eyes.[4]

Ed Wheat

Insight from an older man

I remember a particular evening when I arrived home in a great mood and greeted Cynthia with a kiss while she was at the stove cooking for the twenty-plus people soon to arrive for dinner. From my perspective, she barely offered her cheek and seemed to have a snappy answer to my "How was your day?" Most other times I might have asked if anything was wrong, but I took this apparent response as such a rebuff to my cheery entrance that I simply churned inside, stuffing my feelings of rejection, and then promptly left the room. Right then and there I began building a wall between us, and I became aloof.

Four days later Cynthia pulled me aside and asked what was wrong. Imagine how I felt upon finding out as we talked that she could barely recall our quick exchange— she assured me that she had had no reason to be upset with me and had simply been preoccupied with the tasks at hand.

As I look back on this incident I hope that I learned several lessons about being "embittered." Bitterness blocks intimacy and encourages selfishness to take over. My bitterness was also fed by my neglect of our mutual decision not to let the sun go down on our anger. The real problem was not my anger and other feelings—it was the way I indulged them to satisfy myself. It was not easy for me to admit to Cynthia that anything was wrong, but I am thankful she was willing to approach me.

I've been trying to learn who God wants me to be to Cynthia. He's given me some crash courses in humility, servanthood, and acceptance of valid criticism. But it's the love He has given me for her that makes all the effort and experience worthwhile.

Enjoy life with the woman whom you love all the days of your fleeting life which He has given to you under the sun; for this is your reward in life, and in your toil in which you have labored under the sun.
Ecclesiastes 9:9

Suggested Scripture memory: Colossians 3:19

NOTES
1. Lawrence J. Crabb, Jr., *The Marriage Builder* (Grand Rapids: Zondervan Publishing House, 1982), page 58.
2. Raymond C. Stedman, "Man, the Initiator," in *The Marriage Affair,* edited by J. Allan Petersen, page 80.
3. Oswald Chambers, *My Utmost for His Highest* (New York: Dodd, Mead & Company, 1966), page 212.
4. Ed Wheat with Gloria Okes Perkins, *Love Life for Every Married Couple* (Grand Rapids: Zondervan Publishing House, Pyranee Books, 1980), pages 191-192.

"Let No Unwholesome Word Proceed from Your Mouth"

*Watch the way you talk.
Let nothing foul or dirty come out
of your mouth. Say only what helps,
each word a gift.*
Ephesians 4:29 (Message)

*For the tongue is a pen, which
pressing deeply enough (and
whether for good or for evil) will
write upon the heart.*[1]
Mike Mason

"Workshops on communication teach verbal strategies for sharing and listening in nonattacking and nondefensive styles, but they rarely pinpoint the key problem of selfish motivation. Sharing and listening skills are important to learn, but I rather think that the effort spent teaching the skills could sometimes be better used to persuade people to stop living self-centered lives and to seek first the purposes of God."[2] With these thoughts Larry Crabb diagnoses the fundamental problem of communication in marriage. We can learn helpful skills in communicating, but until our hearts are freed from self and focused on pleasing God, we will not experience truly intimate communication.

Insight into Scripture

1. The root word for communication is *commune*, which means to converse or confer intimately. Carefully read Ephesians 4:20-32 in the context of pleasing God with our communication and answer the following questions.

   a. What is involved in putting on the new self, and how can the new self help in communicating in the right way (verses 20-24)?

   b. Your wife is your nearest neighbor. What can you learn from verse 25 about communicating with her?

   c. What instructions do verses 26-27 provide for communicating negative feelings?

d. What guidelines for conversation can you find in verses 29-30?

e. According to verse 31, what must we put away from our lives in order to speak the truth in love? How can we do this?

f. What is the final admonition in verse 32? Why is it important in communication?

Forgiveness is, at the same time, a pure, supernal giving; the receiver doesn't deserve it; the giver wants nothing for it. It's not a *thanks*giving, because that's the return of one goodness for another. It's not a purchasing price, not even the price of marital peace, because that is hoping to buy one goodness with another. Forgiveness is not a good work which expects some reward in the end, because that motive focuses upon the giver, while this kind of giving must focus completely upon the spouse, the one receiving the gift, the one who sinned. The forgiver cannot say, "Because I have given something to you, now you must give something to me." That's no gift at all.

Rather, forgiveness is giving love when there is no reason to love and no guarantee that love will be returned.[3]

Walter Wangerin, Jr.

2. List the truths for being a good communicator found in the verses below:

Matthew 12:34-35

Galatians 6:1

James 1:19-26

James 4:1

1 Peter 2:21-23

3. a. The Song of Solomon (or Song of Songs) records the communication between Solomon and the Shulammite. Read and meditate on Song of Solomon 2:4,16. This passage is spoken by the Shulammite about Solomon. Why do you think she felt so secure in his love?

b. Read Song of Solomon 4:1-7. In what ways does Solomon express his love to his beloved?

Even before you face your spouse, it is absolutely necessary that you pause and self-consciously surrender the world and all its rights. You drop legalities. You die. Can you in fact do this on your own? Not often and never well. Only Jesus purely whispered from the cross, "Father, forgive them, for they know not what they do." Therefore, it is Jesus who must love you in this step. It is Jesus who frees you from yourself, emptying you of your own will even as once he emptied himself. It is Jesus who divorces you, not from your spouse but from the law, to place you fully under his light of grace. Here your faith, shaped by serious prayer, comes to life, for this is done in trust alone; this is Christ's act and will therefore reveal Christ in your actions. You will demand of your spouse nothing for yourself. Anger has vanished from you; vengeance is gone; love alone is left.[4]

Walter Wangerin, Jr.

Insight into myself

4. a. Are there any obstacles in my heart that I need to lay aside in order to communicate as I should with my wife? If so, what are they and what do I need to do to remove them?

b. Do I have a rein on my tongue? If not, what can I do to begin to bridle my tongue?

c. Can honest prayer become a vital part of my life? How can I ensure that prayer is a priority?

d. How can I instruct my wife to tell me, in an acceptable way, when I hurt or nag her by my speech or actions?

Prolonged anger can kill a marriage—especially when it reflects perceived wrongs from the past that have never been forgiven. Thus, the *love must be tough* concept does not suggest that people become touchy and picky; it does hold that genuine instances of disrespect should be acknowledged and handled within the context of love.[5]

James Dobson

Insight into my wife

5. a. Does my wife feel free to talk with me? Why or why not?

b. Does my wife consider me a good listener? Why or why not?

c. How would I describe my wife's communication style?

d. Have I accepted or understood my wife's way of communicating? Why or why not?

e. How would my wife want me to change in the way I communicate with her?

Because many husbands and wives see no evidence that their ministry can be meaningful to their partners, it is essential that they develop an awareness of their spouse's deepest needs. We can create a climate of noncritical acceptance to encourage our spouses to risk becoming vulnerable. If our partners will not open up, we must realize that because they are made in God's image, deep needs do exist, even if they are well hidden. We must pray for wisdom to know what to do to touch those needs.[6]

Lawrence J. Crabb, Jr.

Insight from an older man

"Oh, I can't believe that I forgot to pick you up! Will you forgive me?" With that simple, honest, heartfelt apology, I thought I had dealt with my mistake.

My "mistake" was that I forgot to pick up Cynthia at a restaurant where she was counseling with a friend. I was involved with my ministry objectives for the evening at church and just drove past the restaurant, oblivious. Eventually, Cynthia came in and sat down next to me in the pew. I smiled, patted her shoulder—totally clueless to any problem! On the way home she very quietly asked me if I remembered that I was to pick her up. In a case like this a man has two options: be pious, or panic! I chose "pious," said the two opening sentences above, and assumed that it was all settled.

I soon discovered, however, that a very important part of the process of forgiveness had been left out. Cynthia verbally forgave me, but the process required more than the mechanics of words. I needed to let her tell me how she felt; I needed to listen carefully even though it was painful to do so. I needed to ask her afterwards if she was "okay" instead of just assuming that my quick apology cancelled out the effect of my oversight. Instead, in my pragmatic view, I figured that since I had confessed and she had said "I forgive you," it was all over and we could go on with life.

Our wives need to know that we care about how they feel and want to understand even when we don't know how or why they "feel that way." Three days after forgetting Cynthia at the restaurant, and after two hours of tea and tears, I learned how Cynthia really felt—it wasn't good. Even the tea was bitter! I told her that I loved her and wanted to understand, and then I tried to listen without being defensive. It wasn't easy. It took a while before she could tell me how much I had hurt her by forgetting her, that she felt she must not be a priority at all in my life. I listened, acknowledged her feelings, and assured her of my love and need of her. And I again asked her to forgive me.

I need to care for and communicate with Cynthia in so many ways. I pray for the Holy Spirit to teach me to be gentle, patient, and loving in all my communication with my wife. God isn't finished with me yet.

> Don't think that friendship authorizes you to say disagreeable things to your intimates. The nearer you come into relation with a person, the more necessary do tact and courtesy become.[7]
> Oliver Wendell Holmes

Suggested Scripture memory: Ephesians 4:29

NOTES
1. Mike Mason, *The Mystery of Marriage* (Portland, Oreg.: Multnomah Press, 1985), page 67.
2. Lawrence J. Crabb, Jr., *The Marriage Builder* (Grand Rapids: Zondervan Publishing House, 1982), page 64.
3. Walter Wangerin, Jr., *As for Me and My House: Crafting Your Marriage to Last* (Nashville: Thomas Nelson Publishers, 1987), page 80.
4. Wangerin, pages 99-100.
5. James Dobson, *Love Must Be Tough* (Waco, Tex.: Word Books Publisher, 1983), page 89.
6. Crabb, page 60.
7. Oliver Wendell Holmes, quoted in *The Marriage Affair,* J. Allan Petersen, ed. (Wheaton, Ill.: Tyndale House Publishers, 1971), page 368.

"They Shall Become One Flesh"

Therefore a man shall leave his father and his mother and shall become united and cleave to his wife, and they shall become one flesh. . . . And the man and his wife were both naked, and were not embarrassed or ashamed in each other's presence.

Genesis 2:24-25 (AMP)

God created this one-flesh experience to be the most intense height of physical intimacy and the most profound depth of spiritual oneness between husband and wife.[1]

Herbert J. Miles

10

"Since the world views sex so sordidly and perverts and exploits it so persistently and since so many marriages are crumbling because of lack of love, commitment, and devotion, it is advantageous to have a book in the Bible that gives God's endorsement of marital love as wholesome and pure."[2] So writes Jack S. Deere about the Song of Solomon. This beautiful book has been interpreted as an allegory, a drama, a lyric poem, a historical record, and a loving illustration of God's relationship with His people. The uniqueness of Scripture is that it is fathomless—and this song, particularly, communicates not only on a spiritual level but also on a practical, human level. The Song of Solomon, along with other scriptures, speaks beautifully and specifically about sex in marriage.

Insight into Scripture

1. In the Song of Solomon God commends to husband and wife the unique intimacy provided by the physical relationship. Take time to read this poetical book carefully (find a translation that outlines the verses by telling who is speaking and what is taking place). As you read, look for some of the key ways that Solomon, the lover, expresses his love for his beloved, the Shulammite.

   a. Summarize how Solomon spoke to the Shulammite.

   b. Write down some of the specific ways Solomon praised his wife on their wedding night (Song of Solomon 4:1-15).

c. Why do you think Solomon spoke like this?

d. How do you think the Shulammite felt toward Solomon?

e. What can you learn from these expressions of love and intimacy about relating to your wife in your physical relationship?

---

2. What does this book teach us about God's view of the sexual relationship? (Look up Hebrews 13:4 as a helpful cross-reference.)

---

3. a. God's original design and intent for the one flesh relationship is found in Genesis 2:21-25. Read these verses and comment on why Adam and Eve were both naked and yet were not ashamed.

b. What do you think hinders us today from experiencing this kind of freedom in the marriage relationship?

But while I am trying to minister to my wife's personal needs, I sense needs within me. It is at this point I must take very seriously the conviction that nearness to God is my only good, that He alone is sufficient to satisfy what I need to live as I should. Upon reckoning what is true—that I am secure and significant in Christ—I must by faith approach my wife as a personally full husband, willing to share the love shed abroad in my heart, needing nothing in return. When she reacts with loving respect, I feel great. When she reacts with something else, like neglect or criticism or indifference, I will hurt—but I must hold firmly onto the truth that I am whole in Christ and therefore not threatened by my wife's response. The more that spouses react to each other on the basis of their perceived fullness in Christ, the more their marriage will progress toward Spirit Oneness.[3]
Lawrence J. Crabb, Jr.

---

4. Proverbs teaches wisdom for daily living in every area of life; the physical relationship in marriage is no exception. Read Proverbs 5:15-23. What instructions and warnings are given to husbands in this passage?

5. The Scriptures clearly instruct a husband and wife in how to relate to one another sexually. Read 1 Corinthians 7:1-5 and consider the following questions.

a. Whose responsibility is it to meet whose needs?

b. In what sense is mutual consideration important for the physical relationship?

c. What conditions are mentioned for refraining from sexual intercourse?

> God steps boldly to the point, finishing any faint-hearted commitment to the sexual relationship once and for all. My body is not mine, but my mate's. I am here to please. Hereafter, to demand rights over my body is to disagree with God's instruction. God makes sex a sacrificial act that is redemptive, in that it gets my eyes off my needs and onto the needs of my mate.[4]
>
> Don Meredith

Insight into myself

6. a. What words describe my current attitudes toward the physical relationship in my marriage?

b. In what ways do I practice or am I willing to practice God's design for sex in our marriage?

c. In what ways am I reluctant to follow God's design, and why?

d. How can I begin to deepen my enjoyment of the one-flesh relationship with my wife?

Husbands, I want you to especially consider this request that Solomon made of Shulmith. He said, "Let me see thy countenance, let me hear thy voice; for sweet is thy voice, and thy countenance is lovely" (2:14).

This speaks of a man who loved to look into his wife's eyes, who loved to talk with her and to hear what she had to say to him. No wonder she became completely secure in his love! As a result of this openness and communication between them, their relationship could grow and mature until it became many-faceted, expressing all the aspects of love that we have discussed in this book. He was her brother, lover, teacher, friend, companion, husband; she was equally everything to him. Their conversation, their lovemaking, their enjoyment in being together became even deeper and richer in quality.[5]

Ed Wheat

Insight into my wife

7. a. How does my wife view me as a sex partner?

    b. How might I deepen my wife's enjoyment of our
       physical relationship?

Talk truthfully, without a hint of guilt or else of criticism, even about sexual difficulties . . . talk as partners who are discussing the third being between you—as parents would discuss a child in need of special care. Then all your talk will be positive, a building up and not a tearing down. It isn't a baby, of course; it's your sex life. But speaking this way, you will be able to handle even heavy things (impotence, frigidity, genital pain, unexpected feelings of anger) without focusing guilt on one or shame on the other—which would divide and silence you after all, and would perpetuate the problem between you. Parents talk very well to share the work of healing a sick child, because together they love that child. Spouses likewise can talk openly, and share their talents, their perceptions, opinions, and their actions to heal a troubled sex life—because *together* they possess that life.[6]

               Walter Wangerin, Jr.

Insight from an older man

The bumper sticker proclaiming "If it feels good, do it," and all the ones that followed it telling us where to do it and who does it better, are a real cultural statement. It is all too easy for us to begin adopting the world's mindset and to think about sex based upon what is suggested to us by bumper stickers rather than upon what is taught us in the Word of God.

God created sex, and we learn the best of His intentions from the Bible, prayer, and growth together in understanding with our wife. Books and therapy may be helpful, but they are no replacement for my commitment to God and my commitment to minister to Cynthia.

I appreciated the thoughts of a romantic actor who said, "A great lover is someone who can satisfy one woman all her life long . . . and who can be satisfied by one woman all his life long. A great lover is not someone who goes from woman to woman to woman. Any dog can do that."[7] My wife is freer to respond to me sexually when she is secure in my unconditional commitment to her and she is secure in my acceptance of her. I certainly want my goals in marriage to be higher than basic instincts for food, sex, and territory.

The Scriptures are clear that God has something great planned for husband and wife. As a man I want to learn how to enjoy the intimacy the Bible speaks about for both of us. I want to establish an atmosphere in which my wife can talk while I listen; in which she can touch and enjoy closeness without my demand for sex. I've found that in this atmosphere of trust and caring I am more satisfied with the intensity and frequency of sex. Like they say of the annual fair in my home state of Texas, our relationship gets better every year!

There are good books to help apply God's principles to our marriages. Some that I recommend are: *Intended for Pleasure*, by Ed Wheat; *The Act of Marriage*, by Tim LaHaye; *Solomon on Sex*, by Joseph Dillow; *Sexual Happiness in Marriage*, by Herbert Miles; and *The Gift of Sex*, by Cliff and Joyce Penner.

I have learned that as I pray with Cynthia, talk with her, and study the Bible with her, we have a much better understanding of God's best for us—and that certainly includes the physical relationship.

> Still, though banished from Eden, the first couple were not banished from one another's arms, nor from the marriage bed. This is one garden to which God continues to welcome husbands and wives, and where they are privileged to return again and again in order to expose their nakedness and to be healed of secrecy and separateness.[8]
> Mike Mason

Suggested Scripture memory: Hebrews 13:4

NOTES
1. Herbert J. Miles, *Sexual Happiness in Marriage* (Grand Rapids: Zondervan Publishing Co., 1967), page 28.
2. Jack S. Deere in *The Bible Knowledge Commentary,* edited by John F. Walvoord and Roy B. Zuck, Old Testament Edition (Wheaton, Il.: Victor Press, 1985), page 1010.
3. Lawrence J. Crabb, Jr., *The Marriage Builder* (Grand Rapids: Zondervan Publishing House, 1982), page 91.
4. Don Meredith, *Becoming One: Planning a Lasting, Joyful Marriage* (Nashville: Thomas Nelson Publishers, n.d.), page 173.
5. Ed Wheat with Gloria Okes Perkins, *Love Life for Every Married Couple* (Grand Rapids: Zondervan Publishing House, Pyranee Books, 1980), page 161.
6. Walter Wangerin, Jr., *As for Me and My House: Crafting Your Marriage to Last* (Nashville: Thomas Nelson Publishers, 1987), page 191.
7. As quoted in Charles R. Swindoll, *Strike the Original Match* (Portland, Oreg.: Multnomah Press, 1980), page 27.
8. Mike Mason, *The Mystery of Marriage* (Portland, Oreg.: Multnomah Press, 1985), page 118.

11

"In the Integrity of My Heart"

*I'm finding my way down the road
of right living, but how long
before you show up?
I'm doing the very best I can,
and I'm doing it at home,
where it counts. I refuse to take
a second look at corrupting people
and degrading things.*

Psalm 101:2-3 (MESSAGE)

*Integrity does not mean that I
am perfect, but it does mean
that I have an honest heart
before God.*[1]

Stephan Tchividjian

LESSON 11 Integrity in business, politics, and even the church is a challenging topic of discussion. Seldom, though, is anything said about integrity in the home. I feel quite strongly that if I cannot be the man God wants me to be within the confines of my home, then I have no valid message or ministry outside my home. Integrity is honesty, uprightness, virtue, goodness, and faithfulness: "the keeping of a commitment after the circumstances under which the commitment was made have changed or deteriorated."[2] Integrity is having a high sense of always wanting to do right and being willing to pay the price to do it.

Insight into Scripture

1. a. "There was a man in the land of Uz, whose name was Job, and that man was blameless, upright, fearing God, and turning away from evil." So begins the book of Job. Job was not perfect, but he did have an honest heart before God. Suffering and under attack from his friends, Job defended his integrity. Carefully read Job 31 and fill in the columns below.

List the ways in which Job lived his integrity	List the proposed consequences of Job's lack of integrity

   b. In what area does Job's life of integrity challenge you?

100

c. Are there some areas in which you can begin to
   increase your integrity? How?

---

2. a. David describes a man of integrity in Psalms 15 and
      26. Read these psalms and write down the character-
      istics of a man who walks in integrity.

   Psalm 15

   Psalm 26

   b. Many of the Proverbs speak of the blameless man.
      Read the following verses and record the benefits of
      integrity.

   Proverbs 2:7

   Proverbs 10:9

   Proverbs 11:3

Proverbs 19:1

Proverbs 20:7

Trust allows him, encourages her, to be naked before you and not ashamed. Naked physically: no part of the body is hidden since no curve of it will be hurt or troubled by embarrassment. Naked emotionally and spiritually: no part of the personality, no feeling, no memory or fear or internal delight need be hidden either, since *nothing* of your spouse will be hurt or abused or embarrassed. Trust allows him, encourages her, to present a whole self before you. And honesty in you, likewise, hides nothing of your whole self from your spouse.[3]

Walter Wangerin, Jr.

Insight into myself

3. a. Is my heart set on doing what is right especially in my home? Why or why not?

b. How do I compromise my integrity in relating to my wife?

c. In what ways am I growing in my knowledge and understanding of Scripture and of God's leading so that I make right and faithful responses in hard situations?

> Reader, how fares it with your family? Do you sing in the choir and sin in the chamber? Are you a saint abroad and a devil at home? For shame! What we are at home, that we are indeed.[4]
> Charles H. Spurgeon

Insight into my wife

4. a. Does my wife trust me in all areas of our life together? Why or why not?

b. How would my wife say I need to change in regard to my living a life of integrity?

> When we speak of integrity as a moral value, it means that a person is the same on the inside as he is on the outside. There is no discrepancy between what he says and what he does, between his walk and his talk. A person of integrity can be trusted, and he is the same person alone a thousand miles from home as he is in church, or in his community, or in his home.[5]
> Billy Graham

Insight from an older man

Integrity is action and attitude based on a firm set of values. Job is a great example of a righteous man who had it all, from prosperity to pain. Job's integrity was present and active before the pain because he feared God—he reverenced the Lord. In the same way, if we are to abide in His tent, if we are to be vindicated by Him, then we must be men of integrity. If we want the Lord to be our shield, if we want to walk securely and leave a godly heritage, then we will choose to walk the blameless path.

Why should we want to become men of integrity? Is it because we desire to be continually transformed into men who honor God with our lives, or is it because we might get caught? If my integrity is based on the person of Christ, I don't have to look over my shoulder or be concerned about what I say in my sleep or be afraid that someone might find out my unfaithfulness in word or deed. I believe that it was Mark Twain who said, "If you always tell the truth, you never have to remember anything!"

It's certainly a challenge to live a life of integrity in today's world—we are definitely out of Eden! But God is faithful: He gives us His Spirit and strength and the way out of temptation (see 1 Corinthians 10:13). It is our choice, however. I, for one, want to reverence God, honor my wife, and demonstrate integrity to my children and to the world in the best way and in the best place—at home.

I will try to walk a blameless path, but how I need your help, especially in my own home, where I long to act as I should.

Psalm 101:2 (TLB)

Suggested Scripture memory: Psalm 15

NOTES
1. Stephan Tchividjian, "The Evangelist's Inner Life," *Decision Magazine,* vol. 29, no. 5 (May 1988), page 12.
2. Unattributed quote from a taped speech by David Jeremiah, "Integrity," given at Forest Home retreat center in California, July 1986.
3. Walter Wangerin, Jr., *As for Me and My House: Crafting Your Marriage to Last* (Nashville: Thomas Nelson Publishers, 1987), page 189.
4. C. H. Spurgeon, *The Treasury of David,* vol. II, part 2 (McLean, Vir.: MacDonald Publishing Co., n. d.), page 240.
5. Billy Graham, "Vision, Integrity, Presence," *Decision Magazine,* vol. 29, no. 10 (October 1988), page 2.

"I Press on Toward the Goal"

*By no means do I count myself an expert in
all of this, but I've got my eye on the goal,
where God is beckoning us onward—
to Jesus. I'm off and running,
and I'm not turning back.*

*So let's keep focused on that goal, those of us
who want everything God has for us.
If any of you have something else in mind,
something less than total commitment, God
will clear your blurred vision—you'll see it yet!
Now that we're on the right track,
let's stay on it.*
Philippians 3:12-16 (MESSAGE)

*Our ultimate goal, our highest calling in life,
is to glorify God—not to be happy. Let that
sink in! Glorifying Him is our greatest pursuit.
Not to get our way. Not to be comfortable.
Not to find fulfillment. Not even to be loved
or to be appreciated or to be taken care of.
Now these are important, but they
are not primary.*

*As I glorify Him, He sees to it that other
essential needs are met . . . or my need
for them diminishes. Believe me, this concept
will change your entire perspective on yourself,
your life, and your marriage.*[1]
Charles R. Swindoll

I often sign off my letters by writing "Keep pressin'!" (based on Philippians 3:14). We do need to be encouraged to press on, to persevere, to keep our eyes on Jesus—to be reminded that our sole purpose is to bring glory to our gracious God. Certainly, life and marriage provide numerous opportunities for the need to keep going, to keep trusting, and to keep "pressin' on."

Insight into Scripture

1. a. Scripture is rich in passages that exhort us to perseverance in our purpose to glorify the Lord. Read the following passages and write down how they encourage your faithfulness.

   1 Corinthians 10:31

   2 Corinthians 4:7-11

   2 Corinthians 4:16-18

   Philippians 3:7-14

   Colossians 3:23-24

Hebrews 12:1-3

b. Which of these scriptures help you the most in continuing to honor God and be a godly husband? Why?

The truth about marriage is that it is a way not of avoiding any of the painful trials and subtractions of life, but rather of confronting them, of exposing and tackling them most intimately, most humanly. It is a way to meet suffering personally, head on, with the peculiar directness, the reckless candidness characteristic only of love. It is a way of living life with no other strategy or defense or protection than that of love. . . . Marriage is a way not to evade suffering, but to suffer purposefully.[2]

Mike Mason

Insight into myself

2. a. As a man who loves God, what is my purpose?

b. As a husband who loves God, what is my purpose?

c. What are my greatest struggles in fulfilling this purpose in my marriage?

d. What are my greatest joys in fulfilling this purpose in my marriage?

e. As I end this study, what is my earnest prayer?

A proper understanding of marriage as a calling to high ministry will cause us to look at the deepest needs of our mates and to appreciate our unique opportunity to touch those needs in significant ways. . . . Christians who have put God to the test by vulnerably surrendering to His will, examining their motives regularly to see where they are protecting themselves rather than ministering, are tasting the goodness of God. These people more and more see their marriage commitment as an opportunity to pursue their deepest desires, to follow a good path and to invite their spouses to walk with them.[3]
Lawrence J. Crabb, Jr.

Insight into my wife

3. a. If there were one thing my wife would want me to do, or stop doing, to honor or please her in a godly way, what would that be? Am I willing to do it (why or why not)?

   b. What is my prayer for my wife?

> The test of the life of a saint is not success, but faithfulness in human life as it actually is. We will set up success in Christian work as the aim; the aim is to manifest the glory of God in human life, to live the life hid with Christ in God in human conditions. Our human relationships are the actual conditions in which the ideal life of God is to be exhibited.[4]
> Oswald Chambers

Insight from an older man

In a world that tells us to "lay back," "cool it," "chill out," the Bible says to "press on," "run with endurance," and "do everything wholeheartedly." This perseverance is a quality of action with a purpose. The Scriptures encourage us to reap the rewards of eternal values now, and not to settle for the world's standard of mediocrity.

You may have seen the illustration of a boy in a pony cart dangling a carrot at the end of a long rod out in front of the pony's nose to keep the pony pulling the cart. There was a time in my life when that picture fit me. I was like that pony, always chasing the carrot of money, prestige, and power—whatever seemed within my reach. I was running very hard for an elusive prize, satisifed enough with each temporary nibble of the "carrot" to stay in pursuit of the whole thing. I was neglecting my family in the process, but I rationalized to myself that everything I was doing was really for them.

Then a friend spoke to me one day about making wise investments. Because he was a wealthy man and a good manager of resources, I listened very closely—hoping for a "hot tip." He gave me a hot tip, all right. He challenged me to invest my life in the only two things that will last forever: the Word of God and the souls of people. He said that I needed to concentrate on my personal walk with God and that my next priority was my family. I've been so thankful for this wise advice, because it has made all the difference in my life. My purpose is "that I may know Him," and my goal for my marriage is that I may love Cynthia and honor her as a joint heir of this wonderful life of grace. To God be the glory! Keep pressin' on!

Jack

It will be worth it all when we see Jesus,
Life's trials will seem so small when we see Christ;
One glimpse of His dear face all sorrow will erase,
So bravely run the race 'til we see Christ.[5]
Esther Kerr Rusthoi

Suggested Scripture memory: Colossians 1:28-29

NOTES
1. Charles R. Swindoll, *Strike the Original Match* (Portland, Oreg.: Multnomah Press, 1980), page 165.
2. Mike Mason, *The Mystery of Marriage* (Portland, Oreg.: Multnomah Press, 1985), page 142.
3. Lawrence J. Crabb, Jr., *The Marriage Builder* (Grand Rapids: Zondervan Publishing House, 1982), page 119.
4. Oswald Chambers, *My Utmost for His Highest* (New York: Dodd, Mead & Company, 1966), page 321.
5. From the hymn "When We See Christ," by Esther Kerr Rusthoi, in *Hymns for the Family of God* (Nashville: Paragon Associates, Inc., 1976), pages 129-130.

BECOME A STRONGER MAN OF GOD.

Becoming a Man of Prayer

Based on Jesus' instructions, this book will
help you achieve a deeper prayer life—starting
with five minutes each day. Experience the joy and
satisfaction that result from a closer connection
with God through honest prayer.

Becoming a Man of Prayer
(Bob Beltz)

Becoming a Man of the Spirit

Designed as a sequel to *Becoming a Man of Prayer*,
this book's seven-week strategy takes you from
minimal knowledge of the Holy Spirit to a clear
understanding of how He works in your life.
Includes discussion questions.

Becoming a Man of the Spirit
(Bob Beltz)

Get your copies today at your local bookstore, by
visiting our website at www.navpress.com, or by
calling (800) 366-7788. Ask for a FREE catalog
of NavPress products. Offer #BPA.

ALSO BY CYNTHIA HEALD

Becoming a Woman of Excellence

Loving Your Husband

Becoming a Woman of Freedom

Becoming a Woman of Purpose

Abiding in Christ

Becoming a Woman of Prayer

A Woman's Journey to the Heart of God

Becoming a Woman of Grace

When the Father Holds You Close

Becoming a Woman of Faith

Walking Together (with Jack Heald)